Pressure Cooker Recipes:

Pressure Cooker Cookbook of Delicious, Fast, Healthy and Easy Recipes

By

Valerie Alston

Table of Contents

Introduction 5

Part 1. How a Pressure Cooker Works 6

Part 2. Browning and De-glazing 8

Part 3. Boiling 12

Part 4. Steaming 14

Part 5. Braising 17

Part 6. Stewing 20

Part 7. Roasting 23

Part 8. Bain Marie (Commonly Known as Pan-in-Pot Method) 26

Part. 9 Cooking Rice 29

Part 10. Extracting Juice 31

Conclusion 34

Thank You Page 36

Pressure Cooker Recipes: Pressure Cooker Cookbook of Delicious, Fast, Healthy and Easy Recipes

By Valerie Alston

© Copyright 2014 Valerie Alston

Reproduction or translation of any part of this work beyond that permitted by section 107 or 108 of the 1976 United States Copyright Act without permission of the copyright owner is unlawful. Requests for permission or further information should be addressed to the author.

This publication is designed to provide accurate and authoritative information in regard to the subject matter covered. This work is sold with the understanding that the publisher is not engaged in rendering legal, accounting, or other professional services. If legal advice or other expert assistance is required, the services of a competent professional person should be sought.

First Published, 2014

Printed in the United States of America

Introduction

Pressure cookers have been around for quite some time. In 1679, a French physicist and mathematician Denis Papin made the first version of the pressure cooker, (though he called it a steam digester at that time) with a large cast iron vessel and a lid that would fit tightly and then could be locked, completely sealing the cooker. In the earlier versions there was no safety valve and once during a demonstration of the pressure cooker it burst and that is how Papin came up with the safety valve.

Over the years pressure cookers have evolved greatly and today we see modernized versions of the earlier pressure cooker, which are smaller in size and much safer to use. Due to an increased safety, they are highly popular amongst chefs. So what exactly is a pressure cooker? It is just a pot with a metal body, which has a special lid, which can be shut so that the steam from the pot cannot escape.

Part 1. How a Pressure Cooker Works

Water boils ate 100°C and on top of a stove the temperature will never go beyond 100°C no matter how high the flame is. But in a pressure cooker the liquid inside the cooker starts to boil and steam is formed. But since the steam has nowhere to go and at the same time more steam is also being generated by the boiling liquid and as a result the internal pressure of the cooker starts to rise. This increase in pressure causes the temperature inside the cooker to rise and it can go up to a maximum of about 121°C. Also since the cooker is sealed tightly and no heat can escape, the boil can also be maintained at this higher temperature inside the cooker. It is this increased temperature, which decreases the overall cooking time and makes people fond of the pressure cooker.

Pressure Cooker Recipes

Pressure cookers are famous worldwide and many people all over the world prefer using a pressure cooker because of the many benefits it has. So different cuisines always have some dishes that can be made with the use of a pressure cooker and they actually turn out to be better than the same dish if it were to be prepared without a pressure cooker.

A pressure cooker can be used to cook almost anything from fruits and vegetables to lentils and different type of meats. In this section we will look at the different ways your pressure cooker will let you cook and then talk about some recipes that can be made using that cooking method.

Part 2. Browning and De-glazing

To brown something is usually the initial step in many recipes like risottos and can be done either before the lid is placed or after it is removed. De glazing is when you add liquid to an extra hot pan so that all the caramelized pieces that are stuck to the pan can be included in the dish as well.

Ragu (Meat Sauce) Recipe

This is a popular recipe amongst many Americans as it is simple and easy to make. Not only that but it can be combined with any pasta or any sort of meat and you will have a proper yummy meal ready in minutes.

Type: Italian Cuisine
Preparation Time: 5 Minutes
Cook time: 15 Minutes
Total Time: 20 minutes

This sauce is best for 16 oz. (500 grams) of any bumpy pasta (like fusilli or penne) so that the meat pieces stick inside and on the outside of the pasta.

Note: Make sure that you start boiling the pasta when you are half way into making your sauce.

Ingredients:

10 Oz (300 grams) of Italian Sausage, which has been removed from its casing

14.5 Oz (400 grams) of chopped tomatoes, either fresh or canned

1 Red Onion

1 Clove of Garlic

A little Fresh Oregano or ½ Tablespoon dry and lightly crushed Oregano

Salt and Pepper (up to taste)

Method:

1. Place the sausage in the cold pressure cooker and turn on the stove on the lowest flame possible. (Do not cover with the lid). For about 4 minutes let the sausage cook on the low flame so that any excess water will evaporate. Soon it will start to sizzle and in the mean time use your cooking spoon (preferably a wooden spoon) to break up the sausage into pieces.

2. Increase the flame from low to medium and now to the pressure cooker add the onions, oregano, garlic

and seasoning. Cook this for about 5 minutes or till the onions have softened. After that, de-glaze your pressure cooker by adding the chopped tomatoes to it and then use your spoon to scrape off any bits that might have stuck to the bottom of the cooker. De-glazing should be done as quickly as possible, so that any liquid from the tomatoes should not evaporate.

3. Add an additional ½ cup to a cup of water in the cooker if your cooker is 6qt or larger. Close the lid and lock it securely afterwards so that you can retain the liquid in the cooker.

4. Now let your pressure cooker stay on the stove on the maximum flame and when it reaches pressure, immediately decrease the flame to the lowest possible and let it cook under pressure for 5 minutes.

5. After the 5 minutes turn, off the heat and remove the cooker from the burner. Open up your pressure cooker when there is no more pressure inside it. (For different pressure cookers there is a different indication for when the pressure has been released from the cooker)

6. Check the consistency of your sauce. If it is too thin (which usually it is) put it back on the stove on a low to medium flame for about 5 minutes without the lid on (so that it simmers). If the sauce is bubbling then that means the heat is too high. Make sure to stir it occasionally and keep on checking the consistency.

7. Once the sauce has reached the consistency of your choice, pour it over your already boiled and drained pasta in a pot and mix well. Garnish with herbs and grated cheese and serve in a plate.

Part 3. Boiling

You can also use your pressure cooker for quickly boiling food with more than half of the water needed. (Water should just cover the food)

Mashed Potatoes

Who doesn't like creamy yummy mashed potatoes? They go so well as side dishes with many main course meals such as steaks and fish. But other than that they are quite delicious on their own as well.

Type: Any (usually used as a side dish)
Preparation Time: 5 Minutes
Cook time: 15 Minutes
Total Time: 20 minutes

Ingredients:

5 to 8 good quality potatoes (scrubbed and washed)

1 tsp. of rock salt (coarse salt is fine as well)

Around 100 ml of cream

Cooking water

Salt and Pepper (up to taste)

Method:

1. Put the potatoes in the pressure cooker and keep on adding water till it reaches half way up to the potatoes. Sprinkle the rock salt on top and then put the lid on and close it tightly. Turn the flame on high.

2. Wait for the pressure to build up, once that happens lower the flame to a minimum flame and let it cook for 15 minutes. Once the 15 minutes are up, remove from the stove and let the cooker cool down and then open it up when there is no more pressure in it.

3. Take out the potatoes and put them in a mixing bowl. (DO NOT THROW AWAY THE WATER, as you will need it later) Let the potatoes cool a bit so that you are able to peel the skin off.

4. After you peel the skin, mash the potatoes and add 2 tablespoons of cooking water followed by 2 tablespoons of cream. Keep on adding the liquids and mashing the potatoes up till your required consistency.

5. Taste the potatoes and adjust the salt and pepper and then serve.

Part 4. Steaming

Steaming is a popular cooking method for retaining all the water-soluble nutrients in the food as when you steam, the food does not come in direct contact with the water but is placed in a steam basket that is then placed in the pressure cooker. In this way, the nutrient content of the food being cooked is retained.

Spicy Cauliflower and Citrus Salad

Another great side dish that is full of flavor and vitamins and goes well with any white meat or fish main course meal.

Type: Italian Cuisine

Preparation Time: 5 Minutes

Cook time: 10 Minutes

Total Time: 15 minutes

Ingredients:

1 Small Cauliflower, with all the florets separated

1 Small Romanesco Cauliflower, with all the florets separated

1-Pound Broccoli

2 Oranges (seedless), skins taken off and sliced thinly

Vinaigrette ingredients:

1 Orange (zest it and then squeeze it)

4 Anchovies

1 Fresh Hot-Pepper, either chopped or sliced

1 tablespoon of Capers, which have already been conserved in salt. (Remember to use them un-rinsed)

4 tablespoons Virgin Olive Oil

Salt and Pepper (up to taste)

Method:

1. Take a container for the vinaigrette and put all the vinaigrette ingredients inside of it. (You can either leave the ingredients whole or chop them up, apart from the hot pepper, which need to be chopped or sliced) After adding all the ingredients, shake the entire container so the ingredients mix well with each other. Put this container aside then.

2. Add 1 cup of water to your pressure cooker and then place a steaming basket inside. To the basket add the

cauliflowers and the broccoli. Put on the lid and lock the cooker.

3. Put the cooker on the burner on high flame and let the pressure build up. Once the pressure builds up, decrease the heat to a minimum and let it cook for 6 minutes.

4. Once the vegetables are all steamed, turn them over into the serving plate and intertwine with the oranges. Take the vinaigrette container, give it one last shake and pour it all over the salad and enjoy your extra healthy extra citrusy salad.

Part 5. Braising

Braising also involves the use of liquid to cook the meat, like in boiling and steaming, the only difference is when you are braising, the meat is only partially immersed in the liquid, unlike in boiling where it is fully immersed or like in steaming where it doesn't come in contact with the liquid at all.

Pork Loin Braised in Milk

This is a delicious main course meal for any pork lover.

Type: American
Cook time: 40 Minutes
Total Time: 40 minutes

Ingredients:

2 Tablespoons Olive Oil

2 Tablespoons Butter

2-Pound Pork (Make sure the pork is in one piece and has some fat on it. Also tie the meat securely)

2-Teaspoon salt

Ground Pepper

3/4th Litre of milk

A bay leaf

Method:

1. Add the butter and oil in the cooker and melt it on medium heat without the lid on. Once melted, add the pork in the cooker with the fat side placed downwards.

2. Cook the pork from all sides, until it changes to a brown color.

3. Add all the seasoning, the bay leaf and the milk in the cooker. The milk should cover half of the pork. Cover the cooker and close the lid. Turn the flame on to high and let the pressure build up and once the pressure has built up, lower the flame and let the pork cook for 30 minutes under high pressure.

4. After the 30 minutes are up, let the pressure release from the cooker and open it up. Take a serving dish and place aluminum foil on it. Take out the pork from the cooker and place it on the foil to rest.

5. When the sauce has cooled down, spoon out as much of the fat you can from it and as well as the bay

leaf. If the sauce is not up to your required consistency, reduce it a bit on the stove.

6. Taste the sauce and make any adjustments in the seasoning you would like.

7. Slice the pork into pieces, place on the serving dish and pour over the warm sauce and enjoy your meal.

Part 6. Stewing

Stewing is another common way of cooking and while traditional stewing takes lots of time, stewing in a pressure cooker is easy and less time consuming.

Coconut Fish Curry

A spicy curry with the flavors of coconut infused in the fish.

Type: Southeast Asian Cuisine

Preparation Time: 5 Minutes

Cook time: 15 Minutes

Total Time: 20 minutes

Ingredients:

1-1.5 pounds (500-750 grams) Fresh Fish Fillets or Steaks, cut into equal sized pieces (If you use frozen fish then make sure it has been thawed)

1 Tomato, chopped into pieces

2 Green Chillies, sliced

2 Medium Onions, sliced

2 Cloves of Garlic

1/8th teaspoon of Ginger Powder

6 Curry Leaves or Basil

1-tablespoon Ground Coriander

2-teaspoon ground cumin

½ teaspoon turmeric

1-teaspoon chilli powder/ hot pepper flakes

½ teaspoon Ground Fenugreek

(Instead of the above mentioned 5 spices you can also use 3-Tablespoons of Curry powder mix)

500 ml un-sweetened coconut milk

Salt (up to taste)

Lemon Juice (up to taste)

Method:

1. Pre-heat the pressure cooker on medium heat and then add a little oil and fry the curry leaves for about a minute until the edges turn golden.

2. Now add the onions, garlic and ginger and keep on frying until the onions soften.

3. Add all the ground spices into the cooker and sauté them for about 2 minutes or until the spices release their aroma.

4. Now take the coconut milk and use it to de-glaze the cooker from the sides and the bottom.

5. Finally add the green chilies, tomatoes and the fish and stir until the fish is covered with sauce. Now put the lid on and lock it and let the pressure build up. Once the pressure builds up, lower the flame and let the fish cook for 5 minutes on low pressure.

6. When the pressure is released, taste the curry and add salt up to taste. Lastly, spritz it with lemon juice and serve.

Part 7. Roasting

A pressure cooker can also be used to roast the meat. Not only does it take less time but also it gives the meat some extra flavor.

Beer Can Chicken

This recipe is quite unique but rest assured that you'll have a whole tender and full of flavor chicken cooked and ready to dig into on your table in around 30 minutes.

Type: American Cuisine
Preparation Time: 10 Minutes
Cook time: 25 Minutes
Total Time: 35 minutes

Ingredients:

3-4 Pound Whole Chicken

1 Small Beer Can

For the braise:

1 Lemon, zested and squeezed

2 Bay Leaves

For the seasoning:

2-Tablespoons Freshly Chopped Sage

2-Tablespoons Freshly Chopped Thyme

2-Tablespoons Freshly Chopped Rosemary

2-Tablespoon Olive Oil

Juice of 1 Lemon

Salt and Pepper (up to taste)

Method:

1. Rinse the chicken thoroughly and let it dry. The neck and the giblets can be used to give the braise some extra flavor so rinse them as well and then cut them off and put them on the side.

2. Mix together the herbs with the olive oil and lemon and then brush it all on the chicken.

3. Now take your pressure cooker and use it to brown your chicken on a medium flame for about 10 minutes. Once the chicken turns the required color, take it out and de-glaze the pressure cooker with $1/3^{rd}$ of the beer and then add 1 bay leaf and half of the lemon zest.

4. Take the other bay leaf and the other half of the zest and place it in the can and then place the can in the middle of the cooker. Place the chicken on top of this beer can and close the lid shut. (If you saved those giblets earlier, put them in the braising liquid before your close the lid).

5. Turn on the flame to high and when pressure has built up, lower the flame and cook for around 20-25 minutes on high pressure.

6. Once cooked and the pressure has been released from the cooker, very carefully take out the chicken and rest it on a serving dish. (At this point, handle the chicken with care, as it will be so tender that the use of rough hands will make it break into pieces)

7. Turn the heat under the cooker on a high flame and reduce the liquid for up to 5 minutes. After that, strain the liquid if you had added giblets to it, otherwise directly pour it over your chicken and enjoy this tender chicken.

Part 8. Bain Marie (Commonly Known as Pan-in-Pot Method)

This too is a great cooking method in which you can cover a heat-resistant bowl (like Pyrex) with aluminum foil and put it in the steamer basket of the pressure cooker and add around a cup of water to the base and let your food item cook then.

Caramelized Apple Crumb Cake

Type: American

Preparation Time: 10 Minutes

Cook time: 20 Minutes

Total Time: 30 minutes

Ingredients:

6 small Apples (cored and sliced) (Do not peel them)

170 grams (3/4th of a cup) melted Butter

1 square of Butter, softened at room temperature

2- Tablespoons of Flour

1/4th Cup of Raw Sugar

Crumb Filing:

150 grams of Dry Bread Crumbs

120 grams Sugar

1- Teaspoon Ginger Powder

1- Teaspoon Cinnamon

½ a Lemon (both for juice and the rind)

Method:

1. First of all prepare the crumb filling by mixing together all the ingredients of the raw sugar crumb filling plus the melted butter. Set this aside.

2. Take a heat resistant container and butter the bottom of it and then sprinkle flour on it and try to form an even layer of the flour and butter on the bottom of the cooker.

3. Now you will start to layer the apples and since later on the bottom will become the top, make sure you carefully layer the apples in a fan shape so that the core of the apples wont show and also so that the layered apples look even.

4. Now on top of the apples, add the crumb mixture and even it out. Again layer the apples and then the

mixture and keep on going until you are left with no more ingredients to layer the container with.

5. When you are done with the layering, cover the container with some tin foil. Now add around a cup or 2 of water in the pressure cooker and put the container in the steamer basket and put the steamer basket in the cooker. Cover and close the lid and turn the flame on high. Once the pressure is reached, lower the heat and cook on high pressure for 20 minutes.

6. After the 20 minutes have passed, turn of the flame and let the cooker release its pressure so that it is safe to open it now. Once you open it, take out the container and remove the tin foil. Put the serving dish on top of the container and flip it upside down and gently lift the container so that the cake is now on the serving dish.

7. Now sprinkle the raw sugar on the top of the cake and place your cake under your ovens broiler for 3-4 minutes or until the entire sugar has melted giving the top of the cake a golden brown color.

Part. 9 Cooking Rice

Another great use of a pressure cooker is that you can use it to fix up a rice dish in minutes.

Arroz Spanish rice

Type: Mexican

Preparation Time: 5 Minutes

Cook time: 15 Minutes

Total Time: 20 minutes

Ingredients:

1-Tablespoon Vegetable Oil

1 Onion, finely chopped

2 cups White Rice

1 cup canned chopped Tomatoes

2 ½ Cups of Water

2- Teaspoons salt

1/8th teaspoon cayyane pepper

1 Teaspoon Oregano

Method:

1. Pre-heat the pressure cooker on medium heat and sauté the onions in the vegetable oil in the cooker for about 5 minutes or till they soften.

2. Then add the rice and sauté them as well for around 3 minutes until some grains start to brown.

3. Now you will add the tomatoes, water and the spices and mix them well and scrape off any rice grain which might have stuck to the bottom of the pan.

4. Cover and close the lid and let the pressure build up, after which reduce the heat and let the rice cook for 4-5 minutes on high pressure. Once that is done let the pressure be released from the cooker.

5. Once the cooker has been opened, mix the rice and then they are ready to be served.

Part 10. Extracting Juice

Not many people know this but you can also use your pressure cooker to extract juices. And once you have extracted the juice, you can simply mix in some sugar and use it as an ingredient for some desserts or even add it to cocktails or water.

Blackberry Italian Soda

Preparation TIme: 5 minutes

Cook Time: 22 minutes

Total time: 27 minutes

Ingredients:

350 grams of blackberries, rinsed thoroughly and then left to air dry

Around 1 cup of White Sugar

1 Bottle of Sparkling Water

1 Lemon cut into slices like coins

Method:

- For Juice extraction

1. In your cooker add 1 cup of water, place the trivet in it, then on that trivet place a heat proof container and finally the steam basket with berries on top of the container.

2. Cover and close the lid and let the pressure build up. Once that happens, let the berries cook for 12 minutes under high pressure. After the 12 minutes have passed turn off the heat and let the cooker cool down.

3. Take out the steam basket as well as the container. In the container will be the juice extract. Make sure you measure how much extract there is.

- To make syrup:

1. After measuring the extract, pour the juice extract into a heavy based pan and add twice the amount of sugar to it.

2. Turn the burner on to a medium flame and constantly stir it until all the sugar has dissolved.

3. Your syrup is now prepared and you can store it in the fridge for 1-2 months.

- Italian Soda:

1. To each serving glass add 1 spoon of syrup and pour in the carbonated water. Put a fancy skewer in the glass with a lemon slice attached to it.

2. Right before drinking, squeeze the lemon into the drink and enjoy your drink.

Conclusion

Many of you must not have been aware of how great a pressure cooker is and what a great impact it can have in your kitchen and on your culinary skills. But as you can see now, a pressure cooker is a versatile kitchen appliance and can be used to make a variety of dishes, not only from the American cuisine but from a variety of cuisines worldwide. From beans and lentils, to fruits and vegetables, to rice and fish and to chicken and beef, you name it and the pressure cooker can cook it and that to within half the normal cooking time.

Actually in a pressure cooker, the food cooks 70% to 90% times faster than on a stove top. This is due to the fact that the lid is tightly sealed and no steam is allowed to evaporate. Other than that, pressure cookers require less heat as well because usually once the cooker reaches its pressure point, then the flame is decreased to a low flame. As a result, using the pressure cooker also turns out to be energy efficient. Another benefit of the pressure cooker is that it retains the nutritional content of the food as now the vitamins do not boil or evaporate away but instead remain sealed in the food. Also since the lid is tightly sealed, no oxygen can enter the cooker either, meaning no oxidation of the nutrients takes place and hence the food ends up having a higher nutritional content then it would have if it were to be cooked in a normal pan. Combine these three benefits together and you will be making much healthier and much tastier food much quicker and in an energy efficient way. So its a win win situation and that is why a pressure cooker should be in an essential item of any kitchen.

Thank You Page

I want to personally thank you for reading my book. I hope you found information in this book useful and I would be very grateful if you could leave your honest review about this book. I certainly want to thank you in advance for doing this.

www.ingramcontent.com/pod-product-compliance
Lightning Source LLC
LaVergne TN
LVHW021744060526
838200LV00052B/3461